Experiments With Motion

SUSAN H. GRAY

Children's Press®
An Imprint of Scholastic Inc.
New York   Toronto   London   Auckland   Sydney
Mexico City   New Delhi   Hong Kong
Danbury, Connecticut

Content Consultant

Suzanne E. Willis, PhD
Professor and Assistant Chair, Department of Physics
Northern Illinois University
DeKalb, Illinois

Library of Congress Cataloging-in-Publication Data

Gray, Susan Heinrichs.
  Experiments with motion/Susan H. Gray.
    p. cm.—(A true book)
  Includes bibliographical references and index.
  ISBN-13: 978-0-531-26346-4 (lib. bdg.)   ISBN-13: 978-0-531-26646-5 (pbk.)
  ISBN-10: 0-531-26346-0 (lib. bdg.)   ISBN-10: 0-531-26646-X (pbk.)
  1. Motion—Experiments—Juvenile literature. I. Title.
  QC127.4.G73 2012
  531'.11078—dc22   2011011971

All rights reserved. Published in 2012 by Children's Press, an imprint of Scholastic Inc.
Printed in China 62
SCHOLASTIC, CHILDREN'S PRESS, A TRUE BOOK, and associated logos are trademarks and/or registered trademarks of Scholastic Inc.

1 2 3 4 5 6 7 8 9 10 R 21 20 19 18 17 16 15 14 13 12

Find the Truth!

Everything you are about to read is true *except* for one of the sentences on this page.

Which one is **TRUE**?

T or F Inertia can be demonstrated by objects at rest.

T or F Many people use perpetual motion machines to save energy.

Find the answers in this book.

3

Contents

THE BIG TRUTH!

The Shoulders of Giants

**Isaac Newton
experiments
with light.**

4

You can try doing all the motion experiments in this book.

Go Skateboarding Day is celebrated every June 21.

Sometimes horse riders learn about motion the hard way.

The Scientific Method

People who ride horses know a lot about motion. They know that if a moving horse stops suddenly, the rider continues moving forward. Many riders know this from experience or from observing other riders. Sometimes scientists are like horseback riders. They learn from **observations**, too. But scientists also do experiments. They use a process called the scientific method. This is a step-by-step method for finding answers.

Horses are among the 10 fastest land animals.

How Scientists Work

This is how the scientific method works. First, scientists gather all the information they can about something. They also make some of their own observations. Next, they think up a question that has not yet been answered about what they are observing. The scientists then form a **hypothesis**, what they believe is the correct answer to the question. It must be a statement that can be tested.

Scientists begin by being curious about why or how something happens.

8

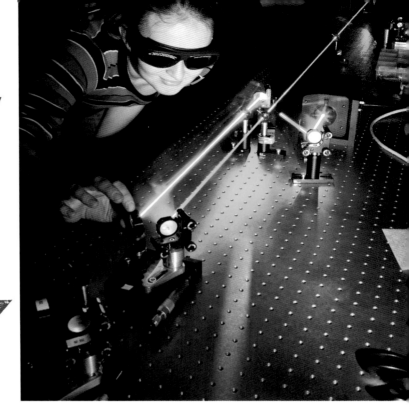

Experiments help scientists learn not only how objects move, but also how energy moves.

Light always moves in a straight line.

Next, they design an experiment to test the hypothesis. During the experiment, they write down everything that happens. Finally, they look at how the experiment turned out and draw a **conclusion**.

Often, it turns out that the hypothesis is correct. Sometimes, though, the hypothesis is not correct. Then they must think up a new hypothesis and design another experiment to test it.

Scientists take careful notes as they experiment.

Being Careful

When scientists do experiments, they work very carefully. They measure things such as the weight, size, and speed of objects they work with. They also **record** everything. They keep track of the steps they take in their experiment and the results they get. This comes in handy later if they want to try the experiment again.

A scientist must also keep an open mind. When an experiment does not turn out as expected, the scientist may be disappointed. However, this is a good time to rethink things. He or she might decide to change something and try the experiment again. No matter what happens, it is an opportunity to discover something new and unexpected.

Trains in China can travel more than 200 miles (330 kilometers) per hour.

Scientists study motion to create high-speed trains.

Motion, Inertia, and Friction

When something changes its position, it is said to be in motion. People riding roller coasters are in motion. So are **skiers** swooping down snowy mountainsides and skaters spinning in circles. Whether they know it or not, they are all following certain laws of motion. In this book, we will learn some of these laws. We will also do some experiments to see how they work.

Some roller coasters go faster than 120 mph (193 kph).

12

Law Number One

The first law of motion has to do with **inertia**. Inertia is the tendency for things to keep doing what they're doing. A ball rolling down a hill will keep rolling until something stops it. A rock sitting on the ground will stay sitting until something moves it. The rolling ball and the sitting rock both have inertia.

More force will be needed to overcome the inertia of the larger rock on the right.

Inertia helps keep a speeding car moving.

The law of inertia says that an object in motion will tend to stay in motion and an object at rest will tend to stay at rest. Objects will keep doing what they're doing until some other force acts on them. You see the law of inertia at work every day but probably don't notice it. So let's do a demonstration of this law. Then we'll set up some experiments to learn more about motion and inertia.

Demonstration: Flying Figures

In this demonstration, we'll show how objects in motion tend to stay in motion.

Materials:

- a wooden plank 6 feet (1.8 meters) long and at least 8 inches (20 centimeters) wide
- a sturdy desk or table about 30 inches (76 cm) high
- a concrete block no more than 3 inches (7.6 cm) thick
- a skateboard
- a plastic action figure or doll; the figure should have jointed arms and legs

Gather up all the materials you need.

Procedure:

1. To make a ramp, rest one end of the wooden plank on the edge of a desk or table.

2. Put the concrete block on the floor at the bottom end of the plank. This keeps the plank from sliding.

3. Put the skateboard at the top of the ramp. Seat the action figure near the front.

4. Release the skateboard.

Steps 1 and 2 set up the ramp you will use in the experiment.

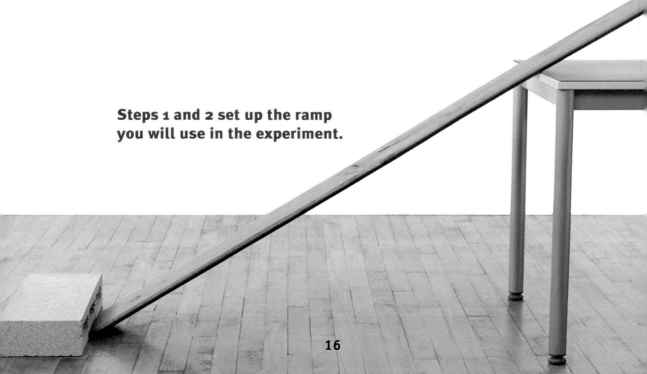

Observe: When the skateboard hits the concrete block, what does the action figure do? What does the back of the skateboard do? After the skateboard stops, what does it do next?

What happened? The action figure and the skateboard both demonstrate inertia. Although the skateboard stopped, the action figure continued moving forward.

Step 3

When the skateboard hit the concrete block, it jumped just a bit. It would have continued moving forward but could not. Instead, some of its momentum was directed upward. Once the skateboard came to a stop, it remained stopped. Its inertia makes it stay that way until another force acts on it.

Skateboarders use inertia to launch themselves into the air.

Experiment #1: Friction at Work

Observe: **Friction** causes a moving object to slow down. Friction can also make it harder for an object to start moving.

Research question: Would friction affect how far the action figure flew?

True Book hypothesis: The figure will fly a shorter distance if there is more friction on the skateboard.

Materials:
- **tape measure**
- **washcloth**
- **2 rubber bands**
- **a wooden plank**
- **a sturdy desk or table**
- **a skateboard**
- **an action figure or doll**

Many of these are the materials used in the demonstration (p. 15)

Gather these materials.

Procedure:

1. Repeat steps 1 through 4 of the demonstration (p. 16).

2. Measure the distance from the figure to the base of the ramp.

3. Center the washcloth on the skateboard and secure it with rubber bands.

4. Place the action figure on top of the washcloth.

5. Repeat steps 1 and 2 above.

Record your results: Compare the two landing distances.

Conclusion: The washcloth added friction. This caused the action figure to move a shorter distance. Does this match your observations? Was the True Book hypothesis correct?

Steps 4 and 5

Experiment #2: More or Less Friction?

Research question: How much friction would other materials add?

True Book hypothesis: Contact paper has less friction than a washcloth or skateboard. The figure will travel a longer distance.

Materials:
- **piece of contact paper**
- **2 rubber bands**
- **a wooden plank**
- **a sturdy desk or table**
- **a concrete block**
- **a skateboard**
- **an action figure or doll**

Many of these materials were used in the demonstration (p. 15)

Procedure: Repeat steps 3 through 5 in Experiment #1 (p. 20), this time using contact paper. Make sure the non-sticky side of the paper faces up.

Record your results: How far did the figure fly?

Conclusion: Friction is greater when a surface is rough. A smooth surface—like the contact paper— creates less friction. As a result, the figure was able to fly farther. Does this match your observations? Was the True Book hypothesis correct?

Remember to write down your hypothesis and your results.

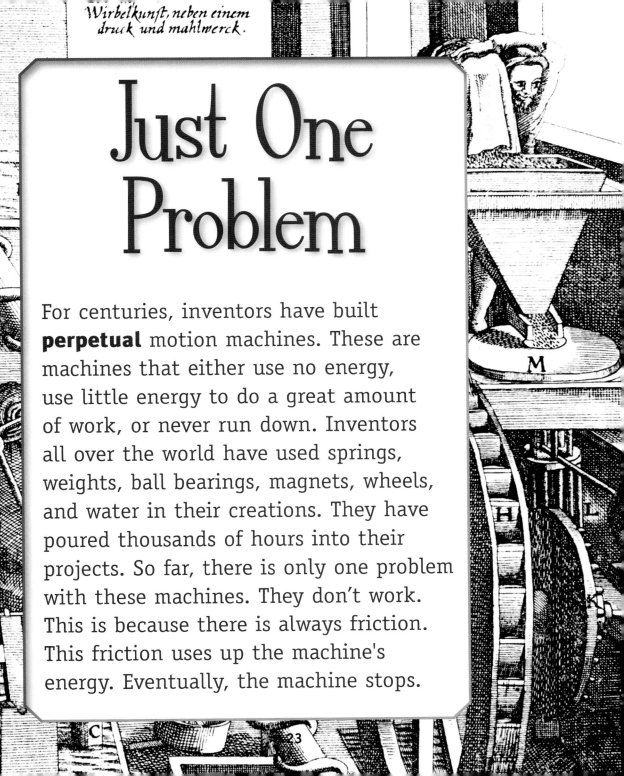

Just One Problem

For centuries, inventors have built **perpetual** motion machines. These are machines that either use no energy, use little energy to do a great amount of work, or never run down. Inventors all over the world have used springs, weights, ball bearings, magnets, wheels, and water in their creations. They have poured thousands of hours into their projects. So far, there is only one problem with these machines. They don't work. This is because there is always friction. This friction uses up the machine's energy. Eventually, the machine stops.

The Shoulders of Giants

Sir Isaac Newton (1642–1727) is known for his discoveries in physics and mathematics. Among his many works are his laws of motion. These laws cover inertia, force, actions, and reactions. Earlier thinkers, such as Galileo Galilei and Leonardo da Vinci, also studied motion. Newton recognized their discoveries and built on their knowledge. "If I have seen further than others," he said, "it is by standing upon the shoulders of giants."

PHILOSOPHIÆ
NATURALIS
PRINCIPIA
MATHEMATICA

Newton's childhood teachers claimed that he was idle and did not pay attention in class.

Newton had many interests, including history and chemistry.

Newton studied rainbows and the properties of light.

CHAPTER 3

Action and Reaction

One of Newton's laws says that for every action, there is an equal and opposite reaction. In other words, when one object pushes another one, it gets pushed back. The push back is just as hard, but in the opposite direction. When you sit in a chair, your body pushes down on that chair. But the chair also pushes up against your body. If the chair were to stop pushing up, it would collapse!

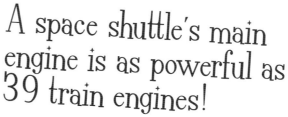

A space shuttle's main engine is as powerful as 39 train engines!

Demonstration: Zoom!

The chair and your body demonstrate Newton's law on objects that aren't moving. Let's do a demonstration to see how the law works on objects that are moving.

Materials:

- **20 feet (6 m) of nylon fishing line**
- **a plastic drinking straw**
- **a balloon**
- **tape**
- **a helper**

You will need someone to help with this experiment.

27

Procedure:

1. Tie one end of the fishing line to a table leg. You can add a piece of tape to the knot to secure it. Thread the other end through the straw.

2. Blow up the balloon and pinch its neck to keep air from escaping.

3. Have your helper tape the straw (on the string) to the side of the balloon, lining it up along the balloon's length.

Step 4

4. Have your helper hold the loose end of the fishing line so it is tight and level.

5. Hold the balloon by the table, then release it.

Observe: What happens to the balloon?

What happened? Air shooting from the balloon's neck is an action. This causes an equal and opposite reaction, sending the balloon scooting along the fishing line.

Step 5

Experiment #1: Line Versus Twine

Observe: Fishing line is smooth, causing little friction.

Research question: How much friction would other materials cause?

True Book hypothesis: The balloon will not travel as far on twine.

Materials:
- **measuring tape**
- **a marker**
- **20 feet (6 m) of twine**
- **nylon fishing line**
- **a plastic drinking straw**
- **a balloon**
- **tape**
- **a helper**

Many of these materials were used in the demonstration (p. 27).

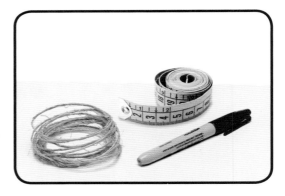

Add these materials to those you used in the previous experiment.

Procedure:

1. Repeat steps 1 through 4 in the demonstration (pp. 28–29).
2. Measure around the inflated balloon. Be sure to inflate the balloon to the same size when you do the experiment again, using twine.
3. Hold the balloon by the table leg and release it.
4. Mark the string where the balloon starts and stops.
5. Repeat all of the steps above using twine instead of fishing line.

Record your results: Did the balloon travel farther on fishing line or twine?

Conclusion: Twine is rougher than fishing line. It creates more friction and slows the balloon down more quickly. The balloon travels a shorter distance. Does this match your observations? Was the True Book hypothesis correct?

Experiment #2: What's Your Angle?

Research question: What happens if the straw is taped to the balloon at an angle?

True Book hypothesis: The balloon will move a shorter distance with the straw taped at an angle.

A Timeline of Motion

2600 B.C.E.
Egyptians oil the ground to reduce friction while dragging building blocks.

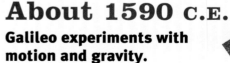

About 1590 C.E.
Galileo experiments with motion and gravity.

Materials:

- **nylon fishing line**
- **a plastic drinking straw**
- **a balloon**
- **tape**
- **measuring tape**
- **a marker**
- **a helper**

Many of these materials were used in Experiment #1 (p. 30).

1687

Isaac Newton publishes his laws of motion.

1957

First human-made satellite is launched into orbit.

Procedure:

1. Repeat steps 1 through 3 for Experiment #1 (p. 31), but tape the straw at an angle.

2. Try the experiment with the straw taped at different angles. Inflate the balloon to the same size each time.

Record your results: When did the balloon travel farthest?

Conclusion: When the straw is at an angle, the balloon spins more and travels forward less. Also, some of the force of the air pushes against the line. The greater the angle, the greater the friction. Does this match your observations? Was the True Book hypothesis correct?

You can try taping the straw at many different angles.

Newton's Second Law

Isaac Newton developed three laws of motion. The first dealt with inertia, and the third had to do with actions and reactions. His second law involved force, **mass**, and **acceleration**. Newton said that a steady, unchanging force pushing an object will cause it to speed up, or accelerate. If the object's mass suddenly doubled, it would speed up only half as much.

Around We Go

You have learned about inertia, friction, actions, and reactions. You have used toys moving along a straight path. Now let's study some special features of circular motion. Do objects moving in a circle or curve behave differently than objects moving in a straight line? Let's do a demonstration to find out.

A tornado is an example of high-speed circular motion in nature.

Demonstration: Falling Peas?

Materials:

- ➤ **bucket with a handle**
- ➤ **enough dried peas or beans to fill the bucket halfway**

Procedure:

For safety, this demonstration and the experiment in this chapter should be done outdoors.

1. Fill a bucket halfway with dried peas.

2. Hold the bucket in one hand and swing it in a circle, up over your head and back down again.

Step 2

Observe: If you swing the bucket fast enough, nothing spills out. This is because of inertia.

What happened? Moving objects tend to follow a straight line. Objects moving in a circular path also want to move in a straight path. The peas stay in the bottom of the bucket because the bucket is moving fast enough. It keeps them from flying off in a straight line.

During the 1920s, there were more than 1,500 roller coasters in the United States.

Some carnival rides are based on this "bucket of peas" idea.

Experiment #1: Spin the Bottle

Observe: Materials stay at the bottom of a container as it swings in a circle.

Research question: What if the container is filled with several substances?

True Book hypothesis: The materials in the container will mix together if the container is swung in a circle.

Materials:

➤ **bottle of Italian salad dressing that stays mixed for a time after being shaken**

➤ **watch or stopwatch**

➤ **about 5 feet (1.5 m) of heavy string**

Gather these materials.

Procedure:

1. Shake the dressing well. Set it on a flat surface.

2. Use the watch to time how long it takes for the different materials to settle back into layers.

3. Double up the string. Wrap the loop end around the neck of the bottle. Make sure you have an adult help you tie the string tightly around the neck of the bottle.

4. Wrap the other two ends of the string snugly around your hand.

5. Shake the bottle again.

6. Lean forward and spin the bottle in a circle parallel to the ground. Be careful not to bump yourself with the bottle.

7. After several spins, look at the dressing.

Record your results: Are the **ingredients** separated or mixed?

Conclusion: When you spin the bottle, the force pulls the denser materials to the bottom of the bottle. This separates the ingredients more quickly than they would sitting on the table. Does this match your observations? Was the True Book hypothesis correct?

What happened? The ingredients in a bottle of Italian dressing have different densities. Atoms are more closely packed together in denser substances. The densest ingredients naturally settle to the bottom of the bottle.

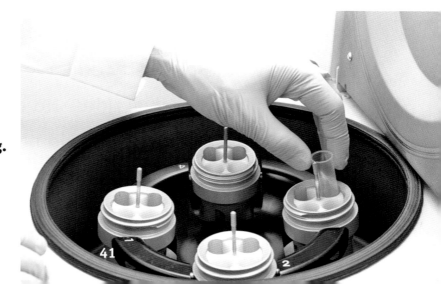

Hospitals use machines that work similarly to this experiment. They spin blood or other substances to separate their contents for testing.

41

Humans have been using skis for at least 9,000 years.

Fun activities such as skiing take advantage of the laws of motion.

Marvelous Motion

Motion always follows certain laws. Without those laws, life would be pretty dull. We would not have skateboards or carnival rides. No one would ice-skate or snow ski. People could not fly in airplanes or launch into space in a space shuttle. Motion is a marvelous thing! ★

Fastest natural movement of air: Tornadoes, such as the 318 mph (512 kph) tornado in Oklahoma in 1999

Speed of the space shuttle: About 5.6 mph (9 kph) while being moved to the launch pad, and 17,600 mph (28,325 kph) while in space

Year of Newton's birth: 1642, the same year Galileo Galilei died

Did you find the truth?

T Inertia can be demonstrated by objects at rest.

F Many people use perpetual motion machines to save energy.

Resources

Books

Atkinson, Mary. *Genius or Madman? Sir Isaac Newton*. New York: Children's Press, 2008.

DeRosa, Tom, and Carolyn Reeves. *Forces & Motion: From High-Speed Jets to Wind-Up Toys*. Green Forest, AR: New Leaf Press, 2009.

Gardner, Robert. *Ace Your Forces and Motion Science Project: Great Science Fair Ideas*. Berkeley Heights, NJ: Enslow Publishers, 2010.

Gardner, Robert. *Forces and Motion Science Fair Projects, Revised and Expanded Using the Scientific Method*. Berkeley Heights, NJ: Enslow Publishers, 2010.

Hollihan, Kerrie Logan. *Isaac Newton and Physics for Kids: His Life and Ideas with 21 Activities*. Chicago: Chicago Review Press, 2009.

Sohn, Emily. *A Crash Course in Forces and Motion With Max Axiom, Super Scientist*. Mankato, MN: Capstone Press, 2007.

Uttley, Colin. *Experiments With Force and Motion*. New York: Gareth Stevens, 2010.

Welch, Catherine. *Forces and Motion: A Question and Answer Book*. Mankato, MN: Capstone Press, 2007.

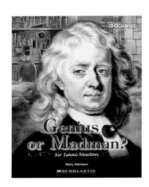

Organizations and Web Sites

Institute of Physics

www.physics.org/explore.asp

Run a search here to find links to many sites explaining the laws of motion.

Newton's Laws of Motion

http://teachertech.rice.edu/Participants/louviere/Newton/index.html

Read about Isaac Newton's life and his laws of motion.

Physics4Kids.com—Motion Basics

www.physics4kids.com/files/motion_intro.html

Visit this site for an introduction to the laws of motion and how they work.

Places to Visit

Children's Museum of Houston

1500 Binz
Houston, TX 77004
(713) 522-1138
www.cmhouston.org

See how simple and complex machines put motion to work.

U.S. Space & Rocket Center

One Tranquility Base
Huntsville, AL 35805
(800) 637-7223 or (800) 63-SPACE
www.ussrc.com

Learn how the laws of motion affect space travel and weightlessness.

Important Words

acceleration (ak-seh-lur-AY-shuhn) — the process of speeding up

conclusion (kuhn-KLOO-zhun) — final decision

friction (FRIK-shuhn) — the force that slows down objects when they rub against each other

hypothesis (hy-PAH-thuh-siss) — a prediction that can be tested about how a scientific experiment or investigation will turn out

inertia (ih-NUR-shuh) — a property of matter by which it remains at rest or continues in the same straight line unless acted upon by some other force

ingredients (in-GREE-dee-uhnts) — materials that make up a mixture of things

mass (MAS) — the amount of physical matter that an object contains

observations (ob-zur-VAY-shuhnz) — facts that are recognized and noted

perpetual (pur-PEH-choo-uhl) — continuing forever

record (rih-KORD) — to write down

skiers (SKEE-urz) — people who ski on snow or water

Index

Page numbers in **bold** indicate illustrations

About the Author

Susan H. Gray has a master's degree in zoology and has done research on plankton and on fish development. She has also written more than 120 books for children. Susan especially likes to write on topics that engage children in science. She and her husband, Michael, live in Cabot, Arkansas.

Friends of the
Houston Public Library